L.B.,

I love y...   !
I thank God for your heart
advice and love! My Goddess
Find Your Tribe Devine!

and Break Bread

Latasha Weatherspoon

Dream In Ink Press
Houston, Texas

Published by Dream In Ink Press
Houston, Texas
Copyright © 2017 by Latasha Weatherspoon

Dream In Ink Press
P.O. Box 550486
Houston, Texas 77255

Printed in the United States of America

Disclaimer: The purpose of this book is to educate and entertain. The author or publisher does not guarantee that anyone following the techniques, suggestions, tips, ideas or strategies will become successful or fully self-aware. While you are completing this book and its activities, if you find yourself faced with emotions you are not equipped to handle, I would advise you to work through them with a professional. The author and publisher shall have neither liability nor responsibility to anyone with respect to any loss or damage caused, or alleged to be caused directly or indirectly by the information contained in this book.

Footprints of the Elders: This book is dedicated to the elder women who have laid down their footprints so that I may find the way.

I come from a line of women
who bounced babies and
balanced budgets at the kitchen
table
so that I could study theory and
debate ideas
in college classrooms.

I come from a line of women
that know the taste of tears
and meals seasoned with
sacrifice
my best life is only an unfitting
offering
placed at my grandmother's feet.

This work is for more than me.
It is for the heroines who planted
little girls
and grew strong women.
Say their names with honor
lining your throat
and reverence on your tongue
Gertie Mae
Gloria
Stella
Patricia
Coleta
Arlene
Marilyn
Angella
Brenda Joyce

When you wrap your lips around
my success
don't forget to mention the
names of the women who held
me under their tongues at prayer
time

Women who worked tirelessly
under the sun
and worried only beneath the
moonlight.
Be sure to mention the women
who whispered
oak tree wisdom and spoke life
to my future
from deep roots

I did not get here alone
I am the product of a long line of
women
who gathered
who cared
who waited
who corrected
who toiled
who taught
who prayed
who learned
who spoke
who sowed
who listened
women who know what it is like
to be both promise and flesh.

You've fixed your eyes on this
life of mine
like the finished product is all
there is to the story
look closer
and you will see those that came
before me
and left lessons like breadcrumbs
for me to follow one unsteady
footstep at a time.

TABLE OF CONTENTS

Book Description

In this refreshingly entertaining and interactive guide, author and acclaimed empowerment coach, Latasha Weatherspoon, serves up easy to digest chapters full of inspiring stories, sage advice, and easy exercises. If you are ready to make serious changes in your life and immediate circle, *Find Your Tribe* is the book for you!

This book is sure to help you to:

> Identify the core principles that drive your life and connections;
> Identify and change the self-limiting beliefs and behaviors that hinder you;
> and it will push you to move past your fears and to step into a new level of confidence. This motivating blueprint will help you learn to love yourself and others, set big goals and reach them - it will basically show you how to create a life you completely love.

When you finish reading this book, you will understand who you are, what your purpose in life is, how to reflect your best self onto those around and how to use your magic to transform the world. If you want to find yourself, live your best life and be surrounded by people who support and encourage you...this book is for you!!

Praise for Find Your Tribe and Break Bread

"Find Your Tribe and Break Bread provided some sound advice on improving your life and who you associate with, in a well-organized manner. Easy to read and apply, it gives self-improvement a turbo boost."

-Kimberlee F.

"This book is amazing! It's the kind of book I wish I read at 21! Its transformative and inspirational."

-   Jayla Pierce

Primer

Why did I write this book?

Every year as a part of my birthday celebration, I plan a community service project. In planning my 2014 project, I surveyed my life and realized that there were so many lessons I did not have to learn on my own. Had someone been in my life to guide me and steer me in the right direction, I would be so much further along than I am. This discovery led me to gather a group of my friends to write letters to girls in child protection services custody.

I asked each one of my friends to tell the girls real life stories of surviving storms and overcoming setbacks that would engrave encouragement into their hearts and minds. When I finished my own letter, I still had so much to say. And so I wrote this book to share the things that I have learned about life and living in hopes that it would make someone else's journey a bit easier. We often lament over what we would have done or should have done in a given situation but the truth is, we cannot change the past, but we can create the future. By being open to share our experiences with others, we serve as a life-raft of safety for those that we encounter.

Keep Going!

I know what it is like to be lonely. You are not alone. Keep going.
I know what it is like to cry. You are not alone. Keep going.
I know what it is like to fail. You are not alone. Keep going.

I know what it is like to feel like there is more to life. You are not alone. Keep going.

I know what it is like to feel stuck. You are not alone. Keep going.

I know what it is like to have a dream deferred. You are not alone. Keep going.

I know what it is like to lose a loved one. You are not alone. Keep going.

I know what it is like to desire connection and understanding. You are not alone. Keep going.

Keep going.

Keep going.

Keep going.

Trust the process!

The journey to finding yourself is not easy, but there is a sense of security that comes from trusting your process that makes it all worth it. As you navigate through this book, find peace in knowing that everything works together for your good; nothing you have been through is wasted. Not one tear you shed was in vain—all of it has a place in your journey. Everything you have lived through has taught you something valuable. Some lessons were to show you places in your life where you need to grow; while others happened to teach you something valuable about the people in your life presently or in your past. No matter the situation, you have been on the path to reaching your breakthrough and you didn't even know it.

When you look at the word *breakthrough* it is important to acknowledge that the word *break* comes before *through.* Sometimes our biggest wins come after our hardest losses. Just when you felt as if you were reaching your breaking point, things changed! You were created to bend, not break. And if you made it through, you are exactly where you were meant to be—right here, right now.

As you go through this book in the pursuit of your personal journey, I want you to remember that before I could write this book, I had to first live through a few things just like you. I had to push past what I saw in order to make it to where I am now. No, it was not easy. But the fact that you are holding my words in your hands lets me know that everything worked out for my good. Whatever you feel right now should serve as confirmation that you are on your way to your next breakthrough. This book requires you to do more than just read it. It requires you to actually do the work of identifying yourself and those you have allowed to become your circle of influence. As you work through the self-illumination activities, just breathe and trust the process. Your body will tell you everything you need to know. If you find yourself taking short quick breaths, your body is telling you that it feels uneasy, so pay attention. The goal is to allow yourself to natural feel what needs to be felt so that you can become aware of your areas of improvement. Inhale peace and calmness, and exhale nervousness.

How to Read this Book

The following guidelines should make it easier to read this book:

- o I have laid out the activities in the way that I feel is best. However, you must go through this process in a way that resonates within yourself.
- o Use the note section to document your thoughts and questions as they arise. It may also be helpful to use a journal or notebook for additional space. Signup online for my newsletter to receive a free copy of the accompanying workbook.
- o Highlight portions of this book that capture your attention. Don't be afraid to write in the margins, use sticky tabs or to do whatever you must to retain the given information.
- o Take this book out into the world with you! Allow this book to become a conversation starter. Talk through your process with others. You may even decide to make it a group effort by starting a discussion group or reading circle. (Your tribe needs this goodness too!)
- o Last but not least, I would love to hear your feedback about your process. So, feel free to email me your thoughts at findyourtribebook@gmail.com.

I am so glad that you have decided to allow me to guide you on your process of self-discovery. Your tribe is waiting on you to get in line. What are you waiting for?

Find Yourself
Part 1: Definition

Part One: Find Yourself

"What do you want?"

There I was, lying on the living room floor of my townhouse, asking myself this same question over and over again. Days before, my friend Jocelyn asked me this one simple question, opening a world of complexities in my mind. "What do you want?" Those four words echoed in my mind like her voice would in an empty room. At the time she asked, I didn't have the answer. All I knew was that I no longer wanted to feel the emptiness I felt day in and day out. The more I thought about it, it became clear to me that I didn't know what I wanted because I barely knew who I was as a person—and as a woman. On the outside, I appeared to be a pillar of strength and security, while on the inside, I was filled with uncertainty and anxiety. What can I say? Just like most people are, I was good at pretending.

In life, we are constantly faced with other people's opinions of who we are and how we should live our lives. When I was in my twenties, the guy I was dating often told me that I was "bossy" and that I should be more "lady-like." The more he said it, the more I believed it. I begin to recall the numerous times that other people said similar things to me. Somewhere along the way, I told myself that if more than one person was saying the same thing about me, it must be true. Slowly but surely, I began to shrink in situations where I should have thrived. I often swallowed my opinion even when it hurt my soul to keep quiet. So many times I allowed the words of others to dictate what I said and how I said it. The person I thought I was had suddenly disappeared.

The Oxford Dictionary defines "self-awareness" as, "the conscious knowledge of one's own character, thoughts, feelings, motives and desires." As we grow through life, encounters with different people often impede our process of learning about ourselves. Having a strong sense of self empowers you to honestly identify your weaknesses, seek improvement and celebrate your strengths through a consciousness of your thoughts, words, and behavior. The answer to the question of identity is fluid and changes as we reinvent ourselves. As we mature mentally, emotionally and spiritually our core values expand to reflect that growth. This suggests that we should consistently question the authenticity of our identity without judgment.

Once I did the work of discovering my identity, I realized that I am not "bossy"—I am a leader. I am task oriented, organized and versed in open communication. Let's be honest, if I were a man, no one would have ever called me "bossy" or suggested I "learn my place." Uncovering who I am and who I was created to be allowed me to rid myself of caving in to the opinions of others. Your value cannot be decided by other people. Until you decide your worth, others will attempt to do it for you.

Illumination Activity 1.0: Define Yourself

The first step in defining who you are is to be confident in who you know you are. Answer the question of who you are today as if you were writing a definition of yourself. Don't just think about the answer to this question, just feel it. Write freely the first words that come to mind. Your definition will change and grow with you, so do not feel boxed into the words you write today. This activity is design as a growth tool. Define yourself a clearly as possible. Do not overthink this process. You have the power to redefine yourself at any time.

Start with the words "I am" or "My name is…"

_____

_____

_____

_____

_____

_____

_____

_____

_____

_____

_____

_____

_____

_____

_____

_____

_____

_____

_____

Critical Critique:

Examine the definition you wrote. What was the root of your definition? Did it stem from negative thoughts or positive experiences?

People who compare themselves to others regularly are more likely to focus on what they perceive as the "lack" in themselves. Comparison is the killer of potential as it can bring feelings of negativity and anxiety. Everybody on earth has to live life on their own terms. No one journey is better than another. Focus on what is on your path and do what you can to make easier for you.

Sometimes you can be your own biggest critic or your own worst enemy. Allowing such negativity to fester inside of you turns your conscious into your personal bully. Your overactive "inner bully" is the part of you that constantly reminds you of your failures, reminds you that you are not "as good as" everyone else, tells you that you are "less than", and it dims the light you carry. Ultimately, it steers you to think less of yourself. When did you allow your inner bully to cower you into a corner? Silence it! Do not give way to the inner bully. It does not honor the creator's presence inside of you nor does it honor your God-given gifts, talents, or unique nature.

The world is filled with the pressures and opinions of others. We allow people to dictate to us what is acceptable and what is not. Social media lifestyles show us the highlights of others' lives and hides the behind-the-scene chaos. We are enamored by what we see and fail to realize it is all a façade. In a world like ours, it is important that we develop solid definitions of ourselves so that we do not fall victim to the "crowd mentality." Take your power back. You are in control. You are the only person who can determine what is best for your life. Learning to love the not-so-loveable parts of yourself just as much as you love the best parts is not easy to do! You are forced to examine how you go through everyday life, how you interact with others and how others interact with you. Loving every part of yourself doesn't happen overnight, it is a process. Trust it.

***Connection*:**

I am a teacher. I am a wife. I am a parent. When most people are faced with the question of who they are; the first thing they do is define themselves by the roles they play in everyday life. Did/Do you define yourself by your everyday roles or titles? Identifying who you are outside of your affiliations and the roles of your life is vital to seeing your value as an individual being. Some people define themselves solely on their career, i.e., "I'm a lawyer," but what you do is not who you are.

This is how people end up feeling lost when they lose their jobs or weather a career shift. Some people define themselves by their memberships, but your affiliation is not your definition. The organizations that garner your membership do not define you at your core, because you were valuable before you paid your membership dues. Other people define themselves by their relationships: "I am Caleb's wife or Addison's mother." Parents are always upset with me when I say that their value is not tied to their children. They were valuable to the world before becoming parents. Mothers especially have difficulty with seeing themselves outside of the confines of motherhood. Children grow up and leave the nest. Does your value decrease when they don't need your constant guidance? Were you not valuable to the world before you became a parent? As precious as our connections are to us, they cannot become what defines us, since the nature of relationships can change, and as well as our roles in them. If your identity is solely tied to your connections, as life progresses your sense of self will suffer. We must do the work to define our value as individuals to be complete enough to give our best to the relationships we cherish.

Illumination Activity 1.1: Re-define Yourself

Let's change things up a bit. I want to guide you in re-defining yourself. Using the following prompts, write a new definition of yourself.

- What individual characteristics of yourself do you hold dear?
- What core values make up your internal foundation (loyalty, courage, security, etc.)?
- How do you want people to remember you?
- What value do you bring to other's lives?
- Who are you at your worst? Who are you at your best?

Describe yourself using the adjectives and behaviors you want the world to associate with you. This doesn't mean that you ignore your areas of improvement, you are simply changing your focus on your internal virtues over your internal deficiencies. When you are finished writing this list, read it aloud—slowly.

_____

_____

_____

_____

_____

_____

_____

_____

_____

_____

_____

_____

_____

_____

_____

_____

_____

_____

_____

_____

_____

_____

_____

_____

How did it make you feel to think about yourself the way you want to be remembered outside of your roles and connections?

_____

_____

_____

_____

_____

To Thine Own Self
Be True

"This above all: to thine own self be true." –William

Shakespeare

Who would have thought that a statement out of Hamlet would still have such a profound meaning in the 21st century? Shakespeare gave us a golden nugget when he reminded us that being true to yourself is vital to your personal success. Being true to oneself is the state of being completely honest and in tune with your needs, desires, and intentions. It is making no apology for who you are as a person and owning your space in the world. This firm stance in life is rooted in an understanding of your value to the world; your self-worth.

You must develop a sense of significance by yourself and for yourself; through honest assessment of your strengths and weaknesses, flaws and beauty, and unique character traits. Understanding that perfection is a myth allows you to cherish all of who you are without the burden of crucifying your uniqueness. This understanding contributes to the development of self-worth. It is the first step to understanding that although you may not look like the models in the magazines but you are worthy of adoration. It is the understanding that you may have made mistakes but you have learned from your shortcomings.

Your self-worth does not change as your life changes. Even when you do not recognize or acknowledge it, your value is present.

External factors like physical appearance, achievement of professional goals, and the opinions of others validate your existence but should not feed into how you see yourself. You set the tone for how others perceive you. Don't be afraid to speak of own your greatness! Being in tune with who you are and not being afraid to let others know is not arrogance, its confidence. Acknowledging the greatness in yourself allows you to recognize it in others.

See yourself. Love yourself. Give love to the world.

Make Peace with Your Scars

As children, our idols were superheroes and heroines like Superman, Wonder Woman and Batman. These beings of superhuman ability carried the weight of the world on their shoulders and made it a better place. You likely imagined having superpowers and pretended to be your favorite character. I dressed up as Wonder Woman so much as a child that it became my father's nickname for me. As adults, we've lost that fascination with heroes but kept our ability to see ourselves as superhuman. We navigate the demands of family, career, and day-to-day obligations with an external smile and internal bruising. We pretend to always be strong and shun away from appearing weak. At what age did we forget that we were merely pretending to be omnipotent? When did we stop dreaming? In the confines of these pages, you do not need the cape. Take it off. Your strength is defined by your ability to be weak. Your perfection is measured by your willingness to face your imperfections. An important part of this journey is making peace with the things you have already survived, so let's make peace with the past.

My Journey:

My mother left me in the hospital shortly after giving birth to me. Although, I was raised by an amazing grandmother and adoring father, I spent much of my youth crippled by the impact of my mother leaving. I've always wanted to be the best at everything I did for as long as I can remember. I've always been well-mannered; and I rarely required discipline for much other than being too inquisitive. I attributed my demeanor to my grandmother's demand for excellence when I was growing up.

However, when looking at myself past the surface, I realize that my desire to be great at everything was to prove I was worthy of love and protection. I used to fear when I did get in trouble that my grandmother would send me away. She never said or did anything to suggest such an idea. In fact, I think she tried to love me into safety. As a young adult, I was still feeling the repercussions of my earliest life experience. My abandonment issues showed up in my friendships, familial and romantic relationships. In my twenties, I struggled with ending relationships and often felt deserted, even when the termination of the connection was in my best interest. To truly heal my heart and define myself from a place of wholeness, I had to first face my brokenness, pick up the pieces, and put them back together from a place of power.

The lessons of the past were remembered without getting stuck in the mental bondage of the process. Everything we experience in life teaches us something. It is up to us to take the lessons and move forward or to fall back. It took me many years and two trips to counseling to recognize that my mother did not leave me because I was not of value; but because she had not done the work to deal with her own past and free herself from the bondage of hurt and desertion. She only gave me, what her mother had given her. We must recognize that our parents are giving us the best and worst of themselves because it is what they have to give. Our parents can be sources of both joy and lamentation. Forgive them, not because they deserve it but because you deserve to be free from the burden of unforgiveness. We will touch on the importance of forgiveness in part two.

******

To be honest about who we are, we must face what we have survived. A lot of our core behaviors are rooted in our childhood experiences and defining relationships. Beliefs about ourselves are directly related to the things we experienced over the course of our lifetimes. Early life experiences are so pivotal. Adverse life experiences lead to damaging belief systems; which ultimately lead to detrimental behaviors in present day. Being neglected, abandoned, or constantly criticized as a child can leave emotional and psychological scars for a lifetime.

Don't be afraid to ask yourself how your scars manifest in your daily life. Spend time investigating your personal journey. Identify how your childhood and significant relationships influence your expectations of yourself and those around you, by paying attention to what was and what is. The more you deny, bury, or reject your scars, the more they will show up in your life. In order to heal your scars, you must acknowledge it, accept it as a part of your journey, then declare your power over it. A person who grew up in an emotionally abusive home may exhibit behavior built around seeking security. A person who didn't receive emotional validation from their parents may be needy in relationships. Examination of past experiences and current behavior patterns will reveal important information about how you see yourself and why you see yourself that way.

Illumination Activity 1.2: Face Your Scars

As you complete this activity, pay attention to yourself. Recognize when you are feeling uneasy by listening to your body. If you begin to feel agitated, or notice tension in your body, it is a clear indicator of negative emotion. Take a clearing breath (deep slow inhale and intentional exhale). If you still feel overwhelmed with emotion, take a break and come back to the activity in a few minutes.

Be open to your healing and remember the covered wounds do not heal. This only a part of your journey. This doesn't have to be a heavy experience but it can have heavy results. Focus on the freedom that will come from releasing unwanted weight. You have proven your strength by beginning this journey. This activity is an opportunity to continue by choosing to free yourself. When you recognize that any discomfort you feel during your growth process is only temporary, you give yourself power over it. Think of this process as a mental/emotional shower. The same way we clean our external bodies, we must actively cleanse our internal beings. Don't linger too much before beginning the activity or you will find a thousand reasons to skip it. It is just like going to the gym; you rarely want to go, but you are always glad you did when it's over.

Definitions:

Damaging Experiences: Things that you have experienced that you haven't let go of from the past, that still affect you in your present life.

Destructive Belief System: The result of negative experiences may be the subconscious root of your actions and not things you actively say aloud. These are often the negative things you think about yourself when you are alone.

Detrimental Behavior: The behavior that result from constant negative thinking (programming). These are the day to day actions that manifest in your life.

Damaging ⟶	Destructive ⟶	Detrimental
Experiences	Belief Systems	Behavior

(Associated Feeling)		
Father Left Home (Abandonment)	I am not worthy of love.	Settling in a relationship
Bullied by Peers (Isolation)	I am ugly.	Becomes anti-social
Overly Criticized by Family (Pressured)	I am not good enough.	Won't apply for a better job because of fear.

Use this chart as a guide to complete the blank chart with your personal experiences, belief systems, and behaviors. Don't forget to breathe through this activity. If you need a minute, take one and return to it later.

Complete the chart below with your answers. Use the chart on the previous page as a guide.

Damaging ⟹ Experiences (Associated Feeling)	Destructive ⟹ Belief Systems	Detrimental Behavior

Illumination Activity 1.3:
Diminishing Blemishes

During this activity, we are going to begin undoing the damage caused by negative thinking, by examining how it shows up in our day-to-day behavior. Use the steps in the chart as a guide to changing the detrimental behaviors that come from our negative thinking and conditioning.

First, recopy the destructive belief systems and detrimental behaviors from activity 1.2. Next, write down a redirecting thought that affirms who you are in a positive manner. This is a proclamation of who you see yourself becoming. Then, consider a positive personality trait (re-visit the list you made in activity 1.1) that displays what you give to the world. Finally, write down an affirming action that is a concrete step to changing your detrimental behaviors. This is a statement of what are you willing to do to shift your energy and change the impact of the things you have experienced. Use the example below as a guide.

Example Chart- Use this chart as your guide.

EXAMPLE Destructive Belief Systems	Detrimental Behavior	Redirecting Thought	Positive Personality Trait	Affirming Action (I Do...)
I am not worthy of love.	Settling in a relationship.	I am complete and deserving of love.	I give love freely.	I choose to love myself and surround myself with people who love me.
I am ugly.	Becomes anti-social	I love myself.	I smile a lot.	I acknowledge my beauty daily.
I am not good enough.	Overworking and anxiety at small mistakes.	I don't need to be perfect.	I can work smart and not hard.	I take time off to reduce my stress.

Fill in with your answers on this page.

Destructive Belief Systems	Detrimental Behavior	Redirecting Thought	Positive Personality Trait	Affirming Action (I Do...)

Find Yourself

Part Two: Forward

Movement

Forgive and Be Forgiven

Centering Thought: "Let go of your past, and your past will let go of you." - Unknown

Once we have identified our adverse experiences, along with the destructive beliefs and behaviors they create, we then have to do the work to shift our thinking to change the negative effects of those situations. In childhood and adolescence, the most difficult part of experiencing adversity is the feeling of helplessness. As we gain greater self-awareness in age, we gain the ability to take our power back. Can we change that it happened? No. But we can change how it impacts us. The things we focus on the most are the things we give life too. Therefore, in order to change our behaviors, we have to change our focus.

Now that you have identified detrimental behaviors that show up in your life, let's examine how we can reshape those behaviors into those that serve your mental and emotional elevation and well-being. In order to fortify yourself, you must first free yourself of things you cannot change. The most powerful way to do this is to intentionally forgive those people and experiences that hurt you in your past.

The following guiding principles are important to your process:

Forgive yourself first. As human beings, we often blame ourselves for the way our lives have turned out. We ask questions like, "What could I have done differently?" and "How could I let this happen?" We assert that in some way, shape, or form, we had a hand in the bad things that have occurred. When we focus on the "should haves" and "would haves" of life, we get paralyzed by regret. In life, we must live through the test before we get the lesson. Take all that you have learned and free yourself from the bondage of hindsight. You cannot change the past, you can only take the knowledge gained and make better decisions. Make a commitment to yourself to honor your growth, by freeing yourself from regret and forgiving yourself first.

Your life is about you. The act of forgiveness is not about the person you are forgiving, but is about freeing yourself from the impact of resentment, hurt, and negative energy. You have to do the work to cleanse your mental and emotional space the same way you do your body. Think of forgiveness as a mental and emotional detox. When we offer forgiveness, we free up heart space that was previously reserved for punishing people who hurt us. When you refuse to forgive, you choose to do the work it takes to stay mad or hurt. Basically, you choose to stay in the negative space by giving up your right to move forward. You are punishing yourself as much or more than the person you are choosing not to forgive! You will be stuck in an emotional prison until you choose to break free. Your freedom is directly tied to your choice to forgive. It is important to recognize that forgiveness is not the same as reconciliation. Choosing to forgive does not mean that you have to choose to restore the assailant to their previous position in your life. Protecting yourself from being hurt repeatedly is within your human rights. Do so with your best interests at the forefront of your actions.

Recognize that it is a process. We live in a world of instant gratification. We expect everything to happen right away. However, matters of the heart don't often work out that way. The choice to forgive is only the beginning. Once you have made the choice in your mind, you have to trust your heart to catch up. When feelings of resentment and hurt start to resurface, you must actively release it again and again until your heart recognizes you have moved past that place. Give yourself permission to feel the emotions when the arise, then actively choose to move on. When thoughts of the past surface in my life, I say aloud, "*I have forgiven this and it has passed.*" This is my mantra to remind myself that I am in control. Once you assert your power over a situation, you will feel the difference the next time you are faced with it. You will feel lighter and less anxious. Trust the process.

Acknowledge your human element. Humans make mistakes, do hurtful things and fall short of expectations. This is a big truth to swallow. The deeper the pain, the harder it is to recover. It is sometimes easy to apply this to yourself and hold it hostage when it comes to others. But guess what? We are all imperfect. This is not to excuse hurtful behavior, but to acknowledge humanity. Extend to others the grace you would like to receive. Most people are only the sum of the experiences they have faced in their lives. My dear friend once told me that, "Hurt people, hurt people." I believe the cycle continues until the choice to heal is made. So, I say "Healed people, heal people." Again, this doesn't mean that you have to actively salvage the relationship or hurtful connection; it only means you wish them peace and healing on their journey instead of harm.

Say it until you live it.

Centering Thought: "When you evaluate your thinking; you can change your thinking. When you change your thinking, you can change your words. When you change your words, you change your life."

The Bible says that life and death are in the power of the tongue. Western philosophy says that your words manifest your reality. No matter what doctrine you subscribe to, the power of the spoken word is acknowledged. The spoken word is the living version of our thoughts—a medium that takes the energy within us out into the world, and sets the course for the universe to respond to us with reciprocal action. It is how we draw both good and bad back to ourselves. I am sure you can think of a time when you had a thought but chose not to say it aloud. Or a time when you were careful to say "I like you" and not "I love you." We censor ourselves because subconsciously we recognize the power of words to cause a reaction. In the same way we expect people to react to our words, we must also expect the universe to react to our words.

God is often referred to as "The Great I AM." We as people were created in His image and likeness. Therefore, everything you say after the words "I am" should reflect the God in you. In the following exercise, you are going to create positive affirmations that honor the God (or positivity) in you through "I am" statements. Positive affirmations are statements that can help you unravel harmful thinking patterns. Positive affirmations are declarations that focus the mind on new truths that support your transition to a more positive state of mind and being. Affirmations are written in present tense. "I am," "I now," and "I have," are often the words used to begin affirmations. Avoid beginning your statements with words like "I will be" and "I am going to," because that leaves your declaration stuck in future tense and not rooted in the present. Framing your declaration in the present tense allows you to see your greatest desires as already attained. Likewise avoid words like "I am not," "I don't," and "I will not," because they place the focus more on the negative action you are shifting away from instead of the one you are moving toward. Positive affirmations work best when they are stated aloud as part of a daily routine. I put a copy of my affirmations in my bathroom mirror so that I see them first thing in the morning. Consistency is vital to the success of an affirmation practice.

Positive Affirmations

I am at peace with my past. I choose to release the past now. I have forgiven myself and others for all hurts, intentional or unintentional. I move forward with a sound mind and calm spirit.

I am grateful for my life. I invite peace and joy into my heart.
I am in control of my life and my emotions. I make sound decisions and trust my ability to bring good to the world.

I now speak life into myself and those around me. I am open to creating new bonds and nurturing my existing ones with reciprocity.

I am productive. I am dedicated to the cultivation of my dreams and the fulfillment of my goals. I now identify and utilize my talents, gifts and resources.

I am beautiful inside and out.
I am loved and loving.
I now give freely of my resources.

Continue to create affirming thoughts:

I am

_____

_____

I am

_____

_____

I am

_____

_____

Continue to create affirming behaviors:

I now

_____

_____

I now

_____

_____

I now

_____

_____

Evolution is Continual

Centering thought: "Perfection is a product of the process."

The journey of finding oneself is constant and ever-evolving. It is not simple, nor is it something that happens overnight. Be patient with yourself. Recognize that as you grow and change, so will your purpose and connections. It is important to commit to continuing to your growth, even when you have a breakthrough. The following are useful practices I have employed on my journey. What worked for me may not work for you, but it's a good place to start. These are practices that helped me build a solid foundation for living a life of abundance. Take all that you feel connected to and integrate it into your evolution process.

Sit with yourself: We live in a world driven by the constant bombardment of bite-sized information. We are forced to consume information quickly, then move on to the next thing. I believe this is one of the greatest drawbacks of the social media age. This constant desire for stimulation feeds restlessness and fear of the quiet moments that allow us to connect with our inner self.

The idea of sitting still and turning off your thoughts will be difficult in the beginning. Everything will be a distraction the moment you choose to be still. You must resist the urge to focus on those things. Over time it will get easier. Make a habit of carving out time to sit with your thoughts and feelings regularly. Listen to your heart;

it will show you the sources of joy and/or chaos in your life. Listen to your body; it will tell you when you are in need of rest. I carve 30-45 minutes in the evening to meditate and recap the day. I treat this time as sacredly as I do work or church. It is my time to turn inward and hear from God. The time of day or length of time does not matter as much as your willingness to be consistent with this practice. You have to find what works for you. Set a short length of time to start with and give your permission to grow as your ability to focus grows.

Be present: Actively being present in your life experiences allows you to both cherish the moments and give your truest self to them. Being present allows you to observe, feel and experience what is going on all around you and inside of you. Nowadays documenting our lives in real time is the thing to do. We video everything and have more pictures than gigabytes of storage. However, don't be so busy documenting that you diminish your ability to experience the moment. Unplug as much as possible, especially when you are surrounded by the people you cherish. Try being social outside of the confines of Facebook, Twitter, and Instagram.

Press pause: When engaged in conversation, listen to comprehend and not to respond. Pausing allows you to attend to the elements of language that are outside of the spoken word. It allows you to empathize with the position of your communication partner. This creates a richer exchange of energy with the people around you. Once you have listened deeply; take a moment to think about how you feel and the words that best convey that feeling. This practice allows you to respond according to your truth and with consideration of your communication partner.

Write about it: Writing allows us to process our thoughts and emotions while keeping us connected to the world around us. Writing can help you pinpoint your inner state of being and creates a record of experiences and the feelings attached to them. It can also be calming and give you a safe avenue to release excess emotion. The experiences we repeat come to teach us something about ourselves. It is up to us to identify the lessons hidden in our patterns. I make it a habit to go back and read my journal periodically to assess my growth. Sometimes my growth is painfully clear, and other times I just have to laugh at myself.

Talk to your tribe: Seek the wise counsel from those who see you for who you are at your core. It is important to surround yourself with people who will tell you the truth about the world's perception of you. It is vital to have a support system that can celebrate the good in you and hold you accountable to improving your personality deficits. We all have times when we wonder how the rest of the world sees us in comparison to how we see ourselves. Use the counsel of your tribe to measure if the things you see in yourself are being projected to the world the same way.

We all are objective and subjective in how we maneuver through the world. An objective community of people is important to development. I love the fact that my *tribe* will get me together when

I need to see myself. They help me to remain humble through honest assessment, but also lift me up when I am not being fair to my own greatness. But! Be very careful to only seek the feedback of people who are genuine and invested in your well-being. When you are growing, there will be people who will try and keep you stuck by reminding you of who you once were. These people are only reminding you of who you use to be because they haven't grown past that place in their own lives. Know that when people are trying to hold you back, it is about their personal insecurity and not because you have "changed." Change is the goal! Make sure that the people in your circle are not only happy about your growth but are doing the work to grow themselves too.

Find your core values: A major part in owning who you are comes from owning what you believe. Each of us should develop a value system rooted in the principles we hold dear. Your core values become a measuring tool used to determine if choices you make are in your best interest. When faced with a decision big or small you should ask if your response is aligned with your values. Choices made in alignment with your core values bring you interpersonal balance and peace. When you find what is important to you, you find your core value system. Consider character traits in yourself and the people you admire.

Take a minute and brainstorm the character traits that are most important to you. Once you have created a list, rank them from most important to least important.

Create your own core values list below.

1.   7.

2.   8.

3.   9.

4.   10.

5.   11.

6.   12.

Once you have a list, consider how these attributes show up in your life and your interactions. Honesty is a value high on my list. Therefore, I am often the person who will tell you the truth. And yes, I hate being lied to. Developing a system is pointless unless you are prepared to implement it. Take hold of you values and do life with them in your focus.

Value	Accompanying Action
Honesty	Gives and expects the truth.
Integrity	Makes decisions rooted in love and reliability.

In order to consistently weigh my actions by my values, I created a mantra around my top three values. Read my mantra, then come up with your own based off your top three values.

My Mantra

"I am clear in my intentions and expectations, so the universe rewards my heart's desire with *honesty*. I give all that I can without bringing harm to my heart, spirit, or personal resources, and in turn I am rewarded with *reciprocity*. I protect my *peace* while allowing myself to experience the best experiences and people the world has to offer."

Your Personal Mantra

_____

_____

_____

_____

Honor your growth

Celebration of your growth allows you to weather the process. As humans, we are gratification driven. When we do not see immediate progress, we begin to justify quitting. However, we must acknowledge all of our wins. Often we are so busy seeking a grand gesture that we miss the little things leading up to it. I believe in acknowledging every lesson learned. Personal development is no exception. The art of reflection is a powerful tool in the passage to elevation. I periodically write letters to the person I evolved from in order to survey my growth. It gives me a clear picture of all the parts of myself. Reflection activities allow us to see what lessons we have learned. Here is an example of one of my letters. Read it. Then pick a time frame and write a letter to your previous self.

A Letter to myself from September 1, 2016 to September 1, 2011

Dear Tasha,

You think moving to Alexandria was a mistake. It was not a mistake. I know you hate it here, but during the nine months you are here, you will learn things about yourself that only this place can teach you. I recognize you are afraid because Baton Rouge holds so much of who you believe you are as a woman. You will become someone different, but that doesn't mean you will be someone worse. You will grow here and the loneliness you are feeling right now is only a growing pain. You need this silence so you can find things within yourself that you don't know are there yet. Some of them are good but some of them need work. It's ok to need work—everyone needs it.

Your family will become even more important to you than they are right now. I know you are mad at your father but you shouldn't be. When he says "I love you" this weekend, say "I love you too." Don't say it because you have to, but because you mean it. You are his everything. You always will be his everything. A lot of things are going to happen to you in the next few months that you will not understand. You will not be prepared. You cannot be prepared. I know you don't know how to let people take care of you yet, it's one of the things this place has come to teach you. When your friends ask you if you are ok, say "no." Do not lie to them because covered wounds heal painfully slower. The next year will remind you that you are a Phoenix. You will feel your heart crack open inside your chest, you will break, but you will not die here; no matter how bad you might want too. You are made to recreate yourself when you're sad and weary. You will survive just like you always have survived. Tasha, remember that God always provides.

The guy you are in love with will break your heart—again. The next time you will leave for good. You will actually move to another state. You will bury yourself in your work. You will convince yourself that you don't want to ever love again. That is only fear talking. There will be men who want to love you. You will not be ready. Don't use them as distractions from your isolation or else you will break their hearts with your bare words and indifferent actions. Say you are sorry when it happens. The apology is not for you. It is for the person who braved the hurricane in your mouth to love you in spite of you. It is for the casualty you experienced in your war with yourself. But don't worry. You will heal and so will they. You will meet a man that restarts your heart. He will be everything you whispered to God in the midnight hour. You will smile for real.

Take care of your body. Never stop running. Taking care of your body is just as important as taking care of your mind. When you gain weight and don't recognize yourself, fight for the image of yourself that you love. Don't allow anyone to turn you against your reflection. Tell anyone who attacks your appearance that this body is not up for discussion. Learn to defend yourself with love.

Everything you have gone through and will go through is not just for you. You will learn how to turn your life lessons into road maps for other people. You will do for them what others have done for you. Don't be afraid to show your scars when the time arrives. They are necessary.

The woman that you have become in these five years is the one you have dreamed about. She is not perfect, but she is in tune with who she is and the universe around her. You will build a pretty amazing life. Live it fully and without hesitation. Live every moment in the moment. I love you and soon you will love you too.

Your Reflection,
Latasha Weatherspoon
2016

Notes:

Find Your Tribe

Part One

Find Your Tribe

The desire for companionship and close connection is human nature. Finding your tribe means attracting a community of people who reflect the qualities you hold dear. This community of individuals is made up of people who bring out the best within us, and they often possess character traits we desire to achieve. The pursuit of authentic connection has been stifled by the shade throwing, and petty parades of reality television and social media spats. During a routine trip to the hair salon, it is not foreign to hear women rehashing the petty, jealous and downright spiteful behavior of cast members on the latest episode of a "reality" show. These images of friendship (frenemy) dynamics are widely consumed, so it is no wonder that many people are uncertain about developing new and lasting bonds. Society tells us that friends are fickle, to say the least. I have often heard people say that they don't need friends, or they only have "associates." This mentality of "I'm a one-person show," is often steeped in the fear of being hurt and rooted in the memory of passed failed friendships or relationships and lack of trust.

The term "tribe" is attributed to the African and Native American cultures, and is used to describe a group of people linked by social, economic, religious, or blood ties, with a common culture and dialect (via The Oxford Dictionary). In life, we often find ourselves in search of a figurative tribe, a community of people to feel at home with. These are the people who celebrate your life on your birthday and on the other three hundred and sixty-four days of the year. They are the ones who show up and support you in everything you do without being asked or asking for anything in return. They are your cheerleaders, prayer warriors, accountability partners, and the reflections of the parts of yourself that you may have kept hidden.

I have been fortunate enough to maintain great friendships throughout my lifetime. Some of them I have known since childhood, others since college, and a few I've adopted in the last few years. No two of friendships are alike, but they all have one thing in common— they love me for real and I love them in return. I have several different tribes of friends that represent people of various ages, life experiences and levels of education. What is true for all of my groups of friends is that we work hard, play hard, and love hard. We all have a desire to connect to a group of people who see us for who we are and love us anyway. This pursuit of unconditional love and acceptance is at the root of the tribal assembly. Like any relationship, friendship takes work. It requires you to make decisions with someone else's best interest in mind. You have to be vulnerable and extend yourself outside of your comfort zone. It requires you to see *love* as an action and not just a word, because you have to actually do the work to develop and sustain a healthy relationship. Say "YES!" to making new friends and "YES!" to gaining an extended community of love, support, and empowerment!

In the "Find Yourself" chapter, you did the work to identify who you are at your core. In this chapter, we are going to look at the character traits you seek in your community of friends. We don't often actually think about what we want from our friends until we aren't getting what we need. In this new season, be proactive about the things you want from the people in your life. Set your intentions and make the universe aware of what you desire from your tribe.

Illumination Activity 2.0: Defining Friendship

Complete the following prompts honestly. In your own words define "friendship." Feel free to continue on additional paper.

Friendship is

_____

_____

_____

_____

_____

_____

_____

_____

_____

_____

_____

_____

_____

Now that you have a personal definition of friendship, let's identify what character traits your friends must have to fulfill your definition. If you could build your perfect friend, what traits would you put inside of them? Be honest but realistic. Don't just enter Beyoncé's name either! This exercise will allow you to see the concrete traits you expect the members of your tribe to possess. Remember that relationships are about reciprocity. So include the things that you are willing to give as well. You cannot expect to receive what you are not willing to give.

Example: My friends are supportive. My friends are honest.

My friends are _____.

My friends are _____.

My friends are _____.

My friends are _____.

My friends are _____.

My friends are _____.

Build Your Tribe

Centering Thought: "We must evaluate those we surround ourselves with; only through honest assessment can we see the root of our connection. Expect the best of yourself and your circle; the universe will respond accordingly."

There are mental, emotional, spiritual, and physiological benefits to friendship. Friendships can serve as a source of healing and stress relief, as well as an avenue for encouragement and accountability. However, you must choose to do the work it takes to build and maintain those deep connections. This starts with recognizing who people are, what they add to your life, and what they take away from it. Over the past few years, I have found myself taking inventory of what people bring to my life. I've been allowing myself to really *see* people. In some cases, I have found my connection deepened based on the consistent love and positive energy they bring. In other cases, this journey has revealed to me that my idea of a person, wasn't who they really were. This process has not been an easy one, but it has allowed me to identify my *tribe*. In the following pages I will share with you some things I find important in building your tribe. This process forces you to be honest about your needs and what you are willing to give. It will also force you to acknowledge the truth of the people you call friends.

Here are some important tips to finding a tribe that reflects your soul:

Be You: Before you can find your tribe you must commit to being honest about who you are. This is the reason the "Find Yourself" chapter comes before the "Find Your Tribe" chapter! It is more difficult to find a community of people that fit your life if you are not being honest about it. If you have to pretend to be something you are not in order to fit in to any assembly of people, they are probably not the best fit for you. Do the things that make you happy and surround yourself with who support your happiness.

Survey Your Circle. This is one of the toughest processes to go through. Some of the people you love the most are not the best for you. The people that we spend the most time with say a lot about who we are. Look closely at your relationships and ask yourself if the people you spend the most time with bring out the best in you. Think about if you were in a crisis, who in your circle would you call? If you were stranded and needed help out of a dire situation, who would you call? If you just landed the job of your dreams, who would celebrate with you without any glimmer of jealousy? Those are members of your tribe.

Ask yourself: Do they support you and encourage me? Do they do their part to foster a positive light in our bond? Would they actively work to repair a rift between us? Do they live up to the definition of friendship I set forth in illumination exercise 2.0?

If the answer is yes, those are members of your tribe. If the answer is no, then they may not be the best fit for your journey.

Recognize that everybody can't come! When you are doing the work of improving your life, you will outgrow some people. The more you began to discover yourself, the more you will learn who fits into your life's plan and who doesn't. It doesn't mean that they are bad people. It just means that they don't fit into your best life. Growing up I always heard people use the "golden rule" as a benchmark for love; "love one another as you love yourself," it says. However, that sometimes is the problem. Some people can't love others because they haven't learned to love themselves. Love is a selfless act that comes from a place of security. Insecure people who have not done the work of learning and loving themselves, will not be able to love you from a place of wholeness. You cannot do the work for them. All you can do is acknowledge what they have shown you, take the lessons they have come to teach you, and move forward with your life.

We have to take people at their actions. No, people are not perfect and you have to recognize when there is room for growth in your connections. However, you also have to acknowledge when a person will not change. Go back to the beginning of this section and ask yourself the same questions about the people you hold dear. If the answer is no; you have to decide if those connections are really what's best for you. Make peace with the fact that you will have to let some people go in order to keep moving forward in your journey. It's a fact that not everyone who comes into your life, comes to stay. It is important to recognize that some people will pass through your life only to teach you a lesson. Don't allow that lesson (no matter how hurtful) to hinder you from creating a lifetime bond with someone else. When you do that, you allow a temporary person to have a permanent impact on your life. Negative energy does not deserve that much power! You have heard the saying a thousand times that people come to your life for a reason, a season, or a lifetime. When their season of connection in your life has come to an end, wish them well and let go. It matters not how long you have been friends—let go. There is more value in quality of years than quantity of years. I would rather have a friend I have only known for two years who has shown themselves as authentic, than have a friend for ten plus years that I have to guess where their loyalty lies.

Make new connections. Once you have surveyed your existing circle; do the work to create new bonds and connections. This means putting yourself into social situations that lead to connecting with like-minded people. If you are a lover of music, go out to hear live bands play. If you are athletic, join a leisure softball league. If you are a poet or lover of poetry, go to open mic night. You get the point. The age of social media makes it easy to connect with like-minded individuals. Join a social group that reflects your interest. Try a new experience and allow yourself to connect with people who are sharing that experience with you. Position yourself to connect with *your* people. Once you are in a conducive environment, extend yourself by initiating a conversation with a new person. Allow yourself to feel the connection. Trust your instincts if you meet someone and feel drawn to them or you just "click," follow that feeling. If it feels effortless and authentic, exchange contact information and grab a coffee later. Learn to invite people into your space. It is the only way to find if they fit into your tribe.

No Shade Zone. You have to ask yourself if you are standing in the way of attracting your tribe. Are you being judgmental and dismissive of people who are trying to connect with you? Sometimes we miss genuine connection based on judgments we make of people on site. Have you ever heard someone say, "When I first met you I didn't like you because, I thought you were stuck up, until I got to know you?" Judgment is at the root of this statement. Give people a chance to show you who they are before you enact preconceived notions. Honor that judgment comes from a place of internal insecurity. Focus on meeting people where they are in their personal journey, and be open to connecting with people who are outside of your normal description of a friend.

Find Your Tribe

Part Two

Maintain Your Tribe

Once you have manifested the members of your tribe, do your part in nurturing and developing those bonds. We often externalize the responsibility for maintaining our connections. However, the truth is like anything else of importance, maintaining friendships take effort.

Here are the things I have found to about fostering camaraderie within your tribe:

Life Happens, adjust. As you grow older, life happens. Everyone has a full calendar of events and overflowing to-do lists. It is easy to make excuses and not be truly present in your relationship with your friends. *Don't make excuses! Make time!* None of us have time to do all the things we want and need to do. However, we can all make the time if we truly want to. You may have to adjust to the demands of your day-to-day requirements, but small acts of love and kindness between friends can go a long way. Send a random greeting card, FaceTime on your lunch break, check in on one another, be present in person when you can, and be honest about when you can't. Allow for change in your friendships as life changes. People will get married, become parents, start new careers, and evolve as time goes on. Our friendships evolve with us.

When my best friend Jocelyn became a mother, our relationship shifted while she adjusted to her new role. She didn't call or answer like she did before my niece was born. During her first year of motherhood, she didn't even know where her phone was in the house!

I missed her terribly. As a result, I adjusted to her lifestyle so that she'd know that I was there for her and still counting her present in my life. I would text her at night or early morning when I knew the baby was settled but she was still awake.

I let her know that when she was free, I would make myself available since I had more freedom. She wasn't just ignoring me, and just as much as I missed her I knew she missed me. We went from talking several times every day to checking in when feasible. You have to be willing to take the first and second step if need be. Friendship, like life, tends to ebb and flow. There will be times where you have to give more in order to sustain the relationship. The key to friendship success is to ensure that you are giving to people who would do the same if the tables were turned.

Adjust to the dynamics of present and make the best effort you can to stay connected. Don't fixate on how your friendship "use to be" and the time you "used" to spend together. Recognize that although life has changed, the reality is that your real friends still love you and are willing to do the work with you.

We all need to recognize the value in our presence. Showing up says to the people we love that "I value you." When I am feeling drained from a long work week and tempted to blow off my friends, I often ask myself the question, *What does this mean to them?* We have to see the value in our presence from an external place. I am guilty of saying, "They will be okay if I'm not there." That statement is a cop out. Don't try to convince yourself that your presence is not needed. I also ask myself, *Would I regret not being present if they were sad I wasn't there?* Life is truly short and we never know when will be our last chance to give love to the ones we call family and friends. If you haven't talked to your friend in a while; call them. If you miss seeing their face, set a brunch date. If you ever catch yourself thinking "Well, I'm not calling because I always call," I challenge you to consider *why* that is the case. Is it a matter of life shifting for the other person or is it that you may be needier than you'd like to admit?

Illumination Activity 2.1: Re-Connect

Name two friends you haven't talked to in far too long.

_____

_____

Make the commitment to do the work and make the first contact.

I will call/contact _____ tomorrow because he/she matters to me.

I will call/contact _____ tomorrow because he/she matters to me.

Love Your Own Way: My grandmother says that you shouldn't expect people to love the same way you do! She is right. Just because they aren't being present the same way you would be, doesn't mean they aren't loving you the best way they know how too. Give the best of who you are and recognize when people are giving you the best they have to offer. Sow the love you want to receive and trust the universe to give you what you need from your friendships in return. This doesn't mean don't hold your friends accountable for not meeting your needs, but instead recognize when they are trying. Open and honest communication allows you to see when a person is being genuine.

Don't Just Be Social Media Friends: Choose touch over technology. The digital world and social media age has made it easy to create pseudo-relationships through empty internet check-ins and status updates. Do the work it takes to actually be social and spend time with your love ones in person when possible. The impact of human contact and face-to-face interaction is priceless. Think of a time when you hadn't seen a friend in a while and you finally run across them. If the interaction was pleasant, you are more than likely going to end it by saying how good it was to see your friend. That feeling of "goodness" cannot be replicated on the computer screen. Take time to put your eyes on the ones you love. It will most likely do you both some good. When you have the pleasure of spending time with your tribe, practice unplugging. Put your cellular device away and be present in the moment. Sometimes we get so caught up in social media that we lose our ability to actually be social.

Talk It Out: Communication is an important tool in any relationship. Openly holding your friends accountable for not being present is an easy way to find out who is really willing to do the work of building lasting connections. Conflict will happen because we are all human beings; but only the committed will take the necessary steps to repair a rift in the relationship. A willingness to restore harmony after a disagreement shows investment. I pride myself on not having any friends that won't talk it out with me.

Take Attendance: All the major landmarks of my life are ornamented with the faces of my friends. Their presence made the happiest times even sweeter and the saddest times bearable. Both times I graduated college and when I won major performance competitions, my friends were there, cheering me on. Likewise, in the days following my father's death, my friends rallied around me without being asked. My dear friends, Carl and Whitney Gilmore, paused their wedding celebration to hold me and make sure that I made it safely to my family from New Orleans, Louisiana to Ville Platte, Louisiana. My best friends, Jocelyn and Alexandra, took off work and literally stayed by my side. On another occasion when I was going through a pretty rough breakup, my dearest friend Alexandra left me a note that read, "When you are falling apart, remember that you have friends to pick up the pieces." These are only a few of the instances where my friends have shown up for me in an insurmountable way. However, when I replay the best and worst times of my life it is clear to me who is always there for me. In the best and worst times of your life, you find out who are your real friends. All you have to do is take attendance.

Iron Sharpens Iron: Our friends should be like a mirror. When we see them, we should see the best of ourselves. There is a saying: "birds of a feather flock together." This means that your friends are the greatest reflection of the person you are and where your life is going. Cherish the people who will believe in you when you face the impossible. Those are the people who are invested in you and will sow into you and your dreams. When I think of the places friendship can take us, I am reminded of the story in the Bible when the paralyzed man couldn't get to Jesus because the door was blocked, so his friends lowered him in through the roof to be healed. Ultimately, this man was healed not because of his faith but because of the faith of the people who surrounded him. Sometimes the faith of the people around us can take us to places we never dreamed. I can vividly remember times in my life where my friends believed in my dreams even when I couldn't even see them clearly. They spoke life to me when I wanted to give up and ultimately shifted my belief in myself. We all need friends with rooftop faith! Friends who work hard on their own dreams and push you to the next level at the same time. Once you find them, love them hard and reciprocate all that they bring to your life.

Be Both The Empty Cup And The Filled Vessel: One of the best things I have ever done was find a mentor and add them to my tribe. Having a mentor is an important step in growing as a person and accomplishing your dreams. A mentor affords you the opportunity to learn from someone else's mistakes and benefit from someone else's successes. However, you must be willing to be an empty cup by removing your ego and allowing someone to pour into your life. Once you have progressed on your personal path, don't forget to reach back and dispense what you have gained from life to someone else. This balance of being filled with knowledge and willingness to learn is critical.

Give Honor Where It Is Due: Tell your tribe what they mean to you. We often wait until a person has gone to glory to express the impact they have had on our lives. In the words of my grandmother, "Give people their flowers while they can still smell them." We need to appreciate the people who show up for us. I use to find myself being so concerned with who wasn't present during my milestones, that I didn't pay the proper honor to those who were. It is easy to get caught in the hurt of absence. One day I realized that everyone has a choice. Everyone gets to choose what and whom is important to them. With this being the case, I chose to shift my focus to the people who were choosing me. Once I changed my focus I realized that while some people were great friends, other people just didn't measure up to what I needed from friendship. It is human nature to focus on the lack in our lives. I challenge you to shift your focus to being grateful for your tribe. You will see immediate return on the gratitude you put into your relationships.

Illumination Activity 2.2: Identify and Honor Your Tribe.

You will create a list of honor, reflecting the things your tribe has brought to your life. Once you have completed this activity, I encourage you to call the people represented and sow your honor into their lives. Continue this list on a separate sheet of paper until you are done.

Example:

Today, I honor <u>Kimberly Lewis</u> for <u>being the friend who always says, "call me if you need me" and means it. She always comes when called</u>.

Today I honor _____ for

_____

_____

_____

Today I honor _____ for

_____

_____

_____

Today I honor _____ for

_____

_____

_____

Today I honor _____ for

_____

_____

_____

Today I honor _____ for

_____

_____

_____

Today I honor _____ for

_____

_____

_____

Today I honor _____ for

_____

_____

_____

Today I honor _____ for

_____

_____

_____

Today I honor _____ for

_____

_____

_____

Notes:

Find Your Dreams

Find Your Dreams

Centering Thought: Dream. Believe. Work.

Dreams are the imaginings that don't seem to go away. They are the conceptions that keep us connected to the assignment of our lives. I believe that each of us are born with a series of assignments we are tasked with bringing to life. That thing inside of you that won't let you rest, won't let you be content in the life you have—THAT is the assignment. Whatever is calling you toward greater in your life is your assignment. When something huge is tied to our purpose, it won't let us go. It is up to us whether or not it becomes one of our greatest successes or one of our greatest regrets. The assignment must get done. We are either going to bring it to life, or we are going to watch as someone else do it. Don't let the whisper inside of you that beckons you toward your dream, grow into a scream of regret.

I believe that God spilled the "imagination potion" into the mold when he created me. As early as I can remember, I've conjured grand ideas of what would become of my life. One Sunday afternoon during my grandmother's weekly bible study, Ms. Mary, our neighbor from across the street, asked me what I wanted to be when I grew up. Instead of answering in a normal nervous child-like tone and walking away; I pushed a footstool into the center of the room, climbed on top and proclaimed, "I'm going to be rich and famous!" I was five years old at the time. When we are children, we are fearless. We see our potential without the haze of fear.

However, dreaming is the easy part. It is the part that doesn't require you to face your fears and insecurities the way that taking action does. It took me many years to realize that fear was the one thing holding me back from accomplishing my dreams. Fear continues to grow, unless you take control over it. My fear of abandonment grew into a fear of rejection, then failure, then a fear of taking risks. There was a point in my life where if I saw someone doing something I wanted to do, I would envy them. I would wonder what I was missing. The truth was, I was missing faith in myself and in my dreams.

Faith by the biblical definition is the substance of things hoped for and the evidence of things not seen. It takes trust to have faith, and you cannot trust anything (including yourself) when you are afraid. Faith and fear cannot coexist. You have to choose which one will rule your emotions and your actions. Don't let the whisper inside of you that beckons you toward your dreams grow into a scream of regret because you are afraid. If the Most-High God plants an assignment inside of you and you neglect it because of fear, you cannot be mad or envious when someone else brings it to pass. The assignment must get done! Each assignment has a purpose that must be fulfilled. It is up to you to choose faith in yourself over fear of failure.

Today, I am the Chief Empowerment Officer (CEO) of The Lifted Lifestyle; an empowerment company that focuses of facilitating mental, emotional and spiritual growth in people across their life span. The first time I planned a workshop was a total act of faith. I prayed that God would guide my thoughts, actions, and vision. I toiled with the idea of hosting my workshop for weeks before I began to take the steps necessary to plan and execute it. I wasn't sure that I was equipped for the task at hand. I was recovering from a painful breakup and was in no position to help others heal. I questioned how could I possibly empower someone else when I didn't always get it right. I was afraid of being judged by those who knew my story.

When the workshop was over, the women in the room gave me feedback about the positive impact of the experience. I knew right then that it was bigger than me. I had found my purpose. I was able to offer the women in the room the healing I found in the preparation. Everything I offered them I had to first live through. Had I not been willing to face my own pain and take the leap of faith, someone else could have missed their restoration. *You have to recognize that not walking in your purpose could hinder someone else from reaching theirs.* You must push through fear so that others can be blessed by your story.

Not long after that first workshop, I completed graduate school. In that same year, I met a ninety-five-year-old man that gave me the words of wisdom I still carry with me today. He told me "Remember this isn't a test run. You don't get a do-over life." I often think of these words when putting off something that I know I should be doing. I don't want to take my unfulfilled dreams to the grave. There are so many people who die with untapped potential for greatness. The only things separating them and us is a choice to do the work it takes to accomplish our dreams. I offer these words to you in hopes that they motivate you as they did me. Take them and make the best of this one life you are given. Chose faith over fear and live your dreams.

I've learned that the only way to climb a mountain or accomplish a dream is one step and one action at a time. Action is the medium that turns dreams into reality. If you want to write a book pick a topic, give yourself a deadline and WRITE! If you want to be a lawyer, study for the LSAT and go to law school. Take your dreams, break them down into short-term goals with deadlines to keep you accountable, then GET TO WORK! Your prosperity exists in the present!

If you focus on maximizing the moment you are in right now, you don't need to worry about the future because it will take care of itself! The future is only a series of present moments strung together. If your focus is on living quality moments in the present, you will change the quality of your life forever!

One of the biggest deterrents to accomplishing your dreams is giving way to fear. Fear is the thief that will rob you of your confidence, clear thinking, and motivation; all of which are needed to take your dreams from concept to reality. Fear is an emotion. Only logic can balance emotion. Here are a few action items I have found useful in annulling fear and its eradicating it at its root:

- *Believe in your abilities.* If you don't believe in yourself, no one else will. If you don't live them out, your dreams will die! There is no way for a seed to grow in unfertile ground. Your faith and belief in yourself creates the space needed for your dreams to grow. There will be moments where your self-belief waivers. In those moments, it is important to have a circle of people that will hold you accountable to your goals and remind you of your strengths.

- **Work even when they don't support you.** There will be people in your life who you believe will support you when you follow your heart and chase your dreams. Work hard even if they do not support you. You have to shift your thoughts, your words, and sometimes the people in your circle in order to succeed! More often than not, the people closest to us have the hardest time seeing our greatness. This has nothing to do with you. Don't lose sleep over it.

- **There is no such thing as the perfect time.** Do not put your dreams off in hopes of beginning your pursuit at the "perfect time." Life does not lend itself to perfect time. There will always be things that come up that will have you feeling as if you should wait to take action. Don't allow life to deter you. There is no better time than the present.

- **Write it down!** The physical act of writing down your goals moves them into a tangible form. Writing your goals down and placing them in a visible place keeps you accountable to them. I place my goals on a cork board next to my bed so they are the last thing I see before bed and the first thing I see in the morning. This constant reminder keeps me focused. Start by taking your dream and breaking it up into short-term, attainable goals. Most of us get overwhelmed at the idea of it all and talk ourselves out of even trying! It's like the old saying, "the only way to climb a mountain is one step at a time." Once you create your short-term goals, give yourself concrete deadlines to get your action items completed. Your goals should resonate within your soul. You should feel deeply connected to them. This ensures that you will not be easily be distracted or swayed from your pursuit. Set goals that connect to your highest sense of self so that you work diligently to achieve them.

- **Set SMART goals:** I have found George T. Doran's SMART system for goal setting to be extremely useful. SMART is an acronym for setting *specific, measurable, attainable, realistic,* and *time-bound* goals.

    o *Specific* - Your goal must be clear and well-defined. Vague or generalized goals are unhelpful because they lack sufficient direction. Be precise in describing your result.

    o *Measurable* - Include precise amounts, dates, and so on in your goals so you can measure your degree of success. Giving yourself benchmarks will allow you to track your success and/or readjust your approach.

    o *Actionable* - Set a sequence of small, attainable action steps that will lead you to your anticipated result.

    o *Realistic* - Your goals should be a balance between requiring hard work and being within reach. It is important to set goals that are attainable in order to protect your morale.

- o *Time-Bound* - Your goals must have a deadline. This allows you an opportunity to assess your progress and celebrate your success. Deadlines are an accountability tool and add urgency to the pursuit of your goals.

- **Prioritize your pursuit.** If you are a person with multiple pursuits, it becomes important to prioritize your goals and how you will approach them. Ranking your goals will help you focus on those that are the most meaningful for you. Consider your investment in your goals when ranking them. How much time will it take? How much money will you have to put up? Which goal gives you the warm fuzzies? Play a little trick on yourself. List the goal you are the most invested in last. This way, you'll stay motivated to keep going until you reach it.

- **Be Consistent.** It is important to set aside time daily to pursue your goals. Even if you cannot complete an action step for your goal each day, you can read or research information relevant to your goals. You have to work as hard on your goals as you do at your day job. The intensity in which you pursue your dreams will be the difference in whether or not you succeed.

Waiting time is not wasted time. The time in which you are waiting and working for your dreams to come true is not wasted. Every moment has a lesson if you look for it. Develop a mindset of rigor that forces you to pursue your dreams like your last breath depends on it. Anchor yourself in positive emotions and remember that everything happens in its rightful time. Just like in pregnancy, you don't know for sure how long you will have to carry a goal before its arrival. Spend your time preparing to live your dreams. Create a space conducive to bringing your dreams to life. When you are in the thick of the process of chasing your goals, there will be times when it feels impossible. Do not be discouraged. Guard your thinking and the way you speak about your dreams, and surround yourself with people that will hold your hand and help you remember your purpose.

Illumination Activity 3.0 Define Your dreams.

Ask yourself the following questions (Answer honestly, feeling the answer deeply.):

What would you do if you believed you couldn't fail?

_____

_____

_____

_____

_____

_____

_____

_____

_____

_____

What idea/dream keeps resurfacing in your spirit? What is the thing that you think about doing in your quietest moments? What would you do if money was no object?

_____

_____

_____

_____

_____

_____

_____

_____

_____

What is keeping you from going after the dream listed above?

_____

_____

_____

_____

_____

_____

_____

Take a moment to envision yourself doing what you envision yourself doing most. Honor the feeling that comes from it.

Illumination Activity 3.1 Plant the Dream

Fill in the chart below with your goals, and the steps you are willing to take to accomplish them. In the same way you have to nurture a plant if you were trying to grow it, you have to nurture your dreams. You have to invest in your goals just as you would plant the seed in good soil then water it, give it sun light and watch it grow. Consider what it takes to grow your dream.

- *Healthy Soil*: Do the work in preparation of achieving your dream. Prepare yourself mentally, physically, and spiritually for the pursuit of your dreams. Find a mentor, ask questions, and make sure that your vision and the reality are one in the same.
- *Water:* Find out what education or credentials may be needed to accomplish your dreams. If education is not warranted, then consider what training is required to ensure your success.
- *Sunlight*: Create an opportunity to live your dream.

Goal (Seed): Become a Certified Life Coach	
List three steps you can take to achieve this goal and the deadline by which you will have the step completed.	
1. **Healthy Soil**	Attend counseling and life coaching sessions with certified professionals to do the work of personal growth. Deadline for completion: Nov. 2013
2. **Water**	Do the research and enroll in a Life Coaching certification program to get training. Deadline for completion: Nov. 2014
3. **Sunlight**	Secure an internship with a trained professional. Deadline for completion: June 2015

Fill in the blanks with your goals:

Goal (Seed): Become a Certified Life Coach	
List three steps you can take to achieve this goal and the deadline by which you will have the step completed.	
1. **Healthy** **Soil**	Deadline for completion: _____
2. **Water**	Deadline for completion: _____
3. **Sunlight**	Deadline for completion: _____

Goal (Seed): Become a Certified Life Coach	
List three steps you can take to achieve this goal and the deadline by which you will have the step completed.	
1. **Healthy** **Soil**	Deadline for completion: _____
2. **Water**	Deadline for completion: _____
3. **Sunlight**	Deadline for completion: _____

Notes:

Break Bread

The phrase "breaking bread" commonly refers to the sharing of a meal as a meaningful social interaction or bonding experience. The expression is rooted in the Bible, as stated in the second chapter of the book of Acts. It states, *"and they continued steadfastly in the doctrine and fellowship, in breaking bread and in prayers. And all that believed were together and had all things in common."* It is with this spirit you should build your life and your tribe, only surrounding yourself with people who are willing to share all of themselves with you and with whom you are willing to share your most precious asset with—your time. Time is the one thing that we cannot buy, or recreate. Give your time only to those who deserve it. Break bread in whatever way is needed at the time. Supporting those who support you, spending money on their businesses, lending a word of comfort during rough times, and showing up for their milestones and important occasions are all ways you can break bread with them. Give to the world as much as you take from it.

Break bread with those you love and those that mean you well. Be reminded that your closest friends are the best reflection of where your life is and where it is headed. It is my sincerest prayer that this work has been beneficial to you. Take what you need from this work and share it with others. Don't let the words of this book be buried here. Take them into your life as seeds and into your fertile soil of meaningful action. This book is only a guide. You must to take the steps needed to make life happen for you and your tribe.

ACKNOWLEDGEMENTS

"Thank you is the greatest gift you can give someone; because it is what you say to God." ~ Maya Angelou

As it is impossible to name every person who has played a part in my life's journey, I am grateful to each and every soul I have come in contact with who has helped me along the way. If you do not see your name written above, it doesn't not mean it isn't written in my heart. Thank you to the many teachers who have shaped my educational and spiritual scholarship. Your dedication to my elevation has created the opportunity for me to share the best of me with the world. Thank you to The Lifted Lifestyle Team for all that you do to bring my vision and our mission to life. To The Lifted Lifestyle clients, thank you for allowing me the privilege of being a part of your path to empowerment. I am humbled by your trust, inspired by your strength and renewed by the God in you.

Thank you to my editing team, Maleeka T. Hollaway and The Official Maleeka Group, LLC., for embodying the spirit of excellence throughout this journey. Your impact is invaluable. Thank you to Jotina Buck for referring me to this literary treasure. Most of all; thank you to every person who thinks my work is worth reading.

IN HONOR OF MY TRIBE
The Board of Directors of My Life

Chazz Bailey	Tejuanna Stegall
Amber Joseph	Shana Burris
Yolanda Doucet	Dinah Riggs
Tiffany Ross	Marc Ward
Hope Dawan	Lasonja Henderson
Tameka Roby	Jai Pierre-Raven
Jessica Cole	Regina Griffith
Jackie Brown	Mercedes Fan Fan
Debra Batiste	Lisa Lemons
Jocelyn Young	Matthew Scott
Nikki Berry	Arlene Richard

Angela Arceneaux   Brenda Moncriffe

Gertie Mae Griffith- My Dear Grandmother "Grand"

Gertie Mae Griffith "My Grand": You are my grandmother and my hero. When I was born you were forty-nine years old. All your children were grown, yet you still found room in your heart and home for me. When people see my work ethic and resolve to be successful, I want them to know that it was planted inside of me by your bare hands. You made little money working as a housekeeper in the small town of Ville Platte, Louisiana, but I didn't know I lived in poverty, because you made sure of it. You made sure that not only was I provided for, but that I also had some of the things I wanted as well. I will never forget how you baked and sold pies to make sure I could be exposed to the same luxuries as my peers. You are God's perfect example of womanhood and motherhood. I can never thank you enough for all you have done for me. I place my best life at your feet as an offering. Your pride in the woman I am is a reward more precious than rubies.

Chazz Bailey: You are proof that God answers prayers. You are everything I prayed for and some things I didn't even know I needed or wanted. When the Southern Baptist church folk say "God will give you double for your trouble," the love you show me has to be what they are referencing. I know I am not the easiest woman to love, but the way you love me with everything in you has made me whole in places I didn't even realize were broken. I could not fly this high without the wind that is your support and encouragement. I love you.

Regina Griffith "My Little Bear": I almost regret putting you on the porch so the stork could come back and get you. I hope that I have been a role model for you. I hope that I have shown you enough of my mistakes that your path was a little bit easier. I hope that you feel protected and cared for the way a little sister should. I hope you understand that I am hard on you because I want the best for you.

Alexandra Jones: There is no question of who I call first when I am at my highest or my lowest. You cheer the loudest when I am winning. You cry the hardest when I am hurting. If I am mad, you are furious! I will never forget the note you left me once that read, "When you are falling apart always remember you have someone to pick up the pieces." You have been my bodyguard and backbone for fifteen years. My family is your family and your family is my family. How did I get so lucky as to have a best friend like you? I don't know but, one thing I do know for sure is I am so glad God allowed our paths to cross. Go Best Friend! Go Best Friend!

Jocelyn Young: I hope that everyone is fortunate enough to have a friend like you. You have been speaking life into my visions and helping me see my purpose clearly since the very beginning of our friendship. You are connected to God on a rare wavelength. I hear him when you speak and see him in your actions. Your heart is always pure and so are your intentions. I would not be all the things I am without you being all the things you are.

Yolanda Doucet: You are one of my oldest friends. You keep me grounded and remind me of all I have overcome to become who I am today. You are a constant reminder of the little blue house on Peach Street that I grew up inside. Thank you for being a warm reminder of home in a cold world.

Arlene Richard: When I was a fifteen-year-old book worm you assured me that there would come a day where I wouldn't feel like such an oddity. You encouraged me to read, write, and trust my talents. I am grateful that God allowed our paths to cross. I needed those words at that time in my life more than you could ever have known. We may not talk much these days, but I want you to know that your place in my journey is one that I value. Your encouragement made projects like this one possible. Thank you.

Angela Arceneaux: You have taken me into your family as one of your children. There is something great to be said for women who give of themselves so willingly. I hope to one day embody the virtues you possess as pillars of strength and resolve. We may not talk often, but one thing I know for sure: wherever you are, you are praying for me, encouraging me, and covering me with words of life. I am grateful for your children for sharing their mother with me.

Brenda Moncriffe: You opened your heart, your home, and your family to me. I have written this paragraph four or five times because I can't seem to find the words to truly express all that you have given me. I am more confident because of your reassurance. I am more loving because of your love. I am more brilliant because of your light. I am more woman because of your example. I am a better human because God saw fit to bless me with your presence. Thank you for mothering me, loving me, and helping me find my way.

Queens Tiffany Ross, Hope Dawan, and Tameka Roby: You all are my sounding boards and confession booths! We share a space that is safe and consecrated. With you women, I can be honest and unfiltered. Our daily conversations span the gamut from scholarly to downright unmentionably hilarious. Your source of honest assessment and objective feedback has been invaluable. Thank you is just not enough.

Amber Joseph: You are my accountability partner. Who is still making friends in their thirties? Me! Who knew that a woman I met in *Black Girls Run* Facebook group, would become one of my dearest friends. Our brief conversations before and after runs turned into consistent support for one another's goals on and off the track. You truly support me in all my endeavors and goals. I appreciate your friendship and encouragement. You never allow me to sell myself short. You hold me to a standard of excellence that is only rivaled by the one my grandmother set. You are in great company and worthy of such comparison.

"Goddess Divine" Jai Pierre-Raven and Lasonja Henderson: You two ladies are truly gifts from God. You both create a space of care and nurturing that fills my heart. I am truly grateful for our sisterhood.

Shana Burris: You are my biggest cheerleader! I often reflect on the offering of love and encouragement that you have sown into my life. When I am having trouble finding my way or remembering my greatness, I use your words as a mirror. That you for seeing in me the things that I sometimes don't see in myself. You are the most talented artist I've ever met and one of the most loving souls to ever live.

Jackie Brown: You share my creative superpowers! You challenge me creatively and you never take "no" for an answer. When I am slacking on producing my art, you call me out on my procrastination. You force me to push the limits of my thinking and creativity. I am forever grateful.

Jessica "Lil Homie" Cole: You were once my mentee. Now, I learn as much from you as you learn from me. You are strength embodied. When I met you many years ago, you reminded me of myself at your age. I was instantly drawn to helping you grow. Who knew all these years letter you would be helping me grow. You help keep me close to the cross.

Nikki Berry, Tejuana Stegall, Dinah Riggs, and Debra Batiste: You four ladies are the older sisters I asked God to send me when I was a child. You tell me the truth, whether I like it or not. You hold me up when I am weak and always steer me in the right direction. Your life lessons and wisdom are priceless. I learned the value of showing my scars to someone who needs to know they can make it from you. I know you love me and I am a better woman because of it. Thank you.

Lisa Lemons and Mercedes Fan Fan: You both are my "Think Tank" partners. I am grateful for the ability to flush out my visions in the safe space you two create. You are always willing to listen and ready to offer advice. When I think of the iron that sharpens me, you two are at the top of the list.

Marc Ward, Matthew Scott, and Phillip Causey, my brothers from other mothers: You allow me to see the male perspective that is often overlooked in our society. You are proof that good men do exist. You are exceptional fathers, brothers, husbands and men who deserve to be honored. Thank you for all that you bring to my life and the world.

Guiding Materials and Recommended Reading

Bourne, E. J. (2010). The Anxiety and Phobia Workbook. Oakland, CA: New Harbinger Publications.

Luna, E. (2015). The Crossroads of Should and Must: Find and Follow Your Passion. New York: Workman Publishing.

Meyer, J. (2014). Living Beyond Your Feelings: controlling motions so they don't control you. New York: FaithWords.

About Latasha Weatherspoon

As an Author, Empowerment Powerhouse, Communications Consultant and Philanthropist, Latasha Weatherspoon is a dynamic speaker and engaging facilitator who inspires audiences all across the nation with her candid and uncanny approach to delivering her audiences with the tools they need most to live a full and successful life.

As Latasha believes that a joyful, loving, abundant and fulfilling life is the right of every human being, her mission is to empower individuals who are on the journey of self-discovery by providing the tools, support and positive reinforcement needed to unearth the truest version of themselves. Weatherspoon is the Chief Empowerment Officer of The Lifted Lifestyle—an empowerment company specifically designed to give the masses the resources, insight and support needed to grow in an environment filled with safety and respect.

In 2014, Weatherspoon received I-10 Media's "40/40 Award"; and she was named one of "Houston's 40

Professionals to Watch Under 40 Years Old" for her work with The Lifted Lifestyle. Her workshops and conferences have drawn capacity crowds in Baton Rouge, Louisiana, Houston, Texas, Atlanta, Ga and more.

Latasha has been commissioned to speak at a variety of events including The Black Girl Excellence Awards, The Survivors with Voices Conference, The U-Matter Learning Center Graduation and many other notable spaces. Her work has been featured in various media platforms including Houston Style Magazine, on the cover of The River and The Word Magazines, All Real Radio's Ren Rising's radio show, on the Houston 97.9 The Box and Magic 102.1's online platforms.

Ms. Weatherspoon is a firm believer in giving back and uses her talents, expertise, leadership and motivation to promote and produce empowerment programming. She hosts a youth entrepreneur event and sponsors a scholarship annually that benefits an emerging young entrepreneur.

Weatherspoon is a graduate of Southern University located in Baton Rouge, Louisiana, where she received both her

Bachelors and Masters of Science in Speech and Language Pathology. She is currently practicing Speech Pathology at her Houston-based communication consulting firm Top Tier Therapy, LLC. Latasha is a certified member of the American Speech-Language and Hearing Association where she holds the Certificate of Clinical Competence (CCC), a nationally recognized credential representing a level of excellence in the field of Speech Pathology.

Stay in touch!

www.LatashaWeatherspoon.com

Facebook.com/LatashaWeatherspoon

Instagram.com/tashaspoon

Twitter.com/tashaspoon

For booking e-mail: Yourliftedlifestyle@gmail.com